PIANO • VOCAL • GUITAR

The Greatest Songs of
BILL & GLORIA GAITHER

D1451976

Cover Photo by T.H. Blevins

ISBN 0-634-07892-5

CORPORATION

7777 W. BLUEMOUND RD. P.O. BOX 13819 MILWAUKEE, WI 53213

Visit Hal Leonard Online at
www.halleonard.com

Preface

Reading over the titles of the songs in this collection is like reading through the journals and scrapbooks of our spiritual formation. For us, each new experience, discovery, failure or growth spurt tended to precipitate a song. Songs were sort of signposts driven into the roadside of our journey.

The particular story line of our life's saga may differ from yours, but we hope the lessons we learned and the discoveries we made will resonate with you, for we know you, too, are pilgrims on a journey.

Some days you may identify with "broken and spilled out"; other days you may feel certain that "something good is about to happen." Wherever you find yourself, we sincerely hope that you will find assurance that *Jesus is Lord of all*, and that He *is* in the process of making *something beautiful of your life*.

You are loved,

Gloria Gaither

Contents

ABIDE IN ME

Words by GLORIA GAITHER
Music by WILLIAM J. GAITHER and CHRIS CHRISTIAN

BECAUSE HE LIVES

Words by WILLIAM J. and GLORIA GAITHER
Music by WILLIAM J. GAITHER

3. And then one day I'll cross that river;
   I'll fight life's final war with pain;
   And then as death gives way to vict'ry,
   I'll see the lights of glory and I'll know He reigns.

THE CHURCH TRIUMPHANT

Words by WILLIAM J. and GLORIA GAITHER
Music by WILLIAM J. GAITHER

BROKEN AND SPILLED OUT

Words by GLORIA GAITHER
Music by BILL GEORGE

COME, HOLY SPIRIT

Words by WILLIAM J. and GLORIA GAITHER
Music by WILLIAM J. GAITHER

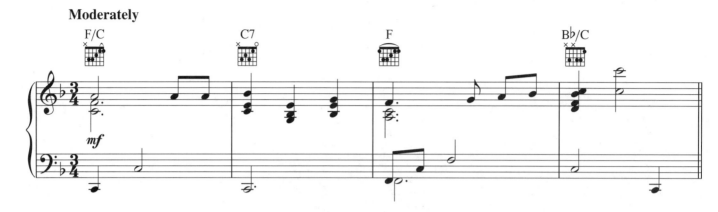

Come as a wis-dom to chil-dren,
Come as a rest to the wea-ry,
Come like a spring in the des-ert,

come as new sight to the blind.
come as a balm for the sore.
come to the with-ered of soul.

THE FAMILY OF GOD

Words by WILLIAM J. and GLORIA GAITHER
Music by WILLIAM J. GAITHER

I'm so glad I'm a part of the fam-'ly of God! I've been washed in the foun-tain, cleansed by His

blood. Joint heirs with Je - sus as we trav - el this

sod, for I'm part of the fam - 'ly ___ the fam - 'ly of

God. ___
You will no - tice we say broth - er ___ and
From the door ___ of an orph - 'nage to the

sis - ter ___ 'round here. It's be - cause we're a fam - 'ly ___ and these
house of ___ the King, no ___ long - er an out - cast, ___ a ___

To Coda ⊕

GET ALL EXCITED

Words and Music by
WILLIAM J. GAITHER

Get all ex-cit-ed, go tell ___ ev-'ry-bod-y that Je - sus

Christ is King. __ I said, get all ex-cit-ed, go tell ___ ev-'ry-bod-y that

Je - sus Christ is King. __ I said, get all ex-cit-ed, go tell ___

HE STARTED THE WHOLE WORLD SINGING

Words by GLORIA GAITHER
Music by WILLIAM J. GAITHER and CHRIS WATERS

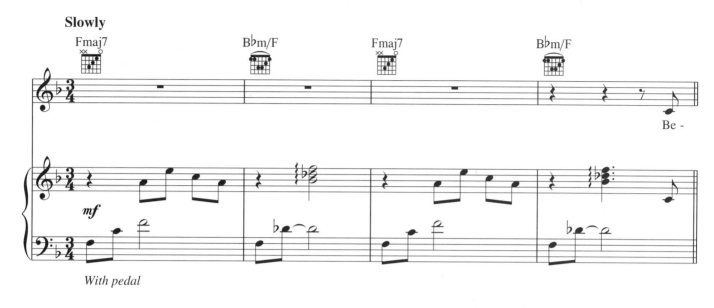

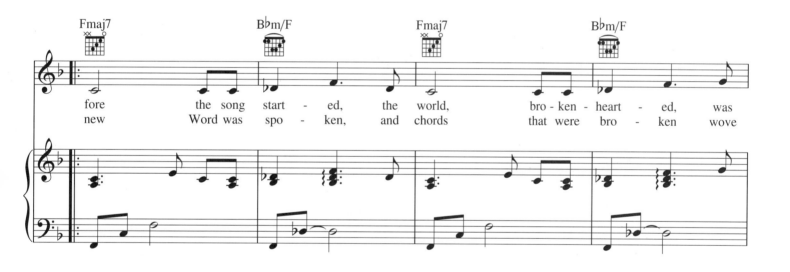

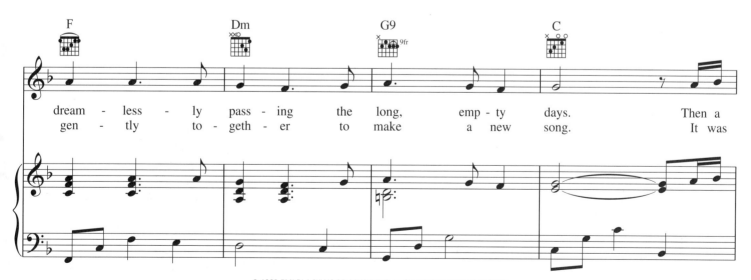

HE TOUCHED ME

Words and Music by
WILLIAM J. GAITHER

With an easy flow

Lyrics:

Shack - led by a heav - y bur - den _____ 'Neath a load of
Since I met this bless - ed Sav - ior _____ Since He cleansed and

guilt and shame _____ Then the hand of Je - sus
made me whole _____ I will nev - er cease to

touched me _____ and now I am no long - er the same. _____
praise Him _____ I'll shout it while e - ter - ni - ty rolls. _____

I AM A PROMISE

Words by WILLIAM J. and GLORIA GAITHER
Music by WILLIAM J. GAITHER

I AM LOVED

Words by WILLIAM J. and GLORIA GAITHER
Music by WILLIAM J. GAITHER

I BELIEVE IN A HILL CALLED MOUNT CALVARY

Words by WILLIAM J. and GLORIA GAITHER
and DALE OLDHAM
Music by WILLIAM J. GAITHER

There are things as we trav- el this earth's shift- ing
lieve that the Christ who was slain on the
lieve that this life with its great mys- ter-

sands that tran- scend all the rea- son of man.
cross has the pow- er to change lives to- day.
ies sure- ly some- day will come to an end.

I COULD NEVER OUTLOVE THE LORD

Words by WILLIAM J. and GLORIA GAITHER
Music by WILLIAM J. GAITHER

I JUST FEEL LIKE SOMETHING GOOD IS ABOUT TO HAPPEN

Words and Music by
WILLIAM J. GAITHER

I WILL PRAISE HIM

Words by GLORIA GAITHER and JOHN W. THOMPSON
Music by JOHN W. THOMPSON

I WILL SERVE THEE

Words by WILLIAM J. and GLORIA GAITHER
Music by WILLIAM J. GAITHER

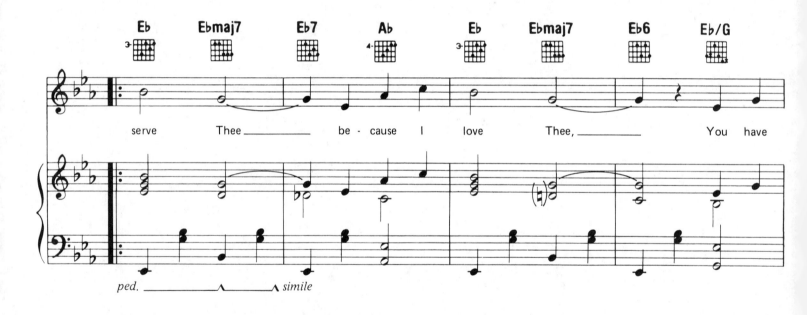

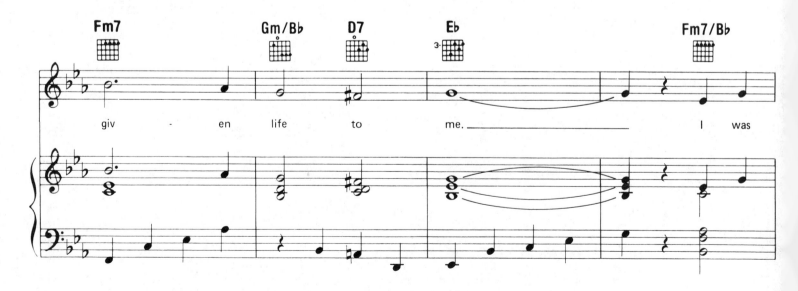

IT IS FINISHED

Words by WILLIAM J. and GLORIA GAITHER
Music by WILLIAM J. GAITHER

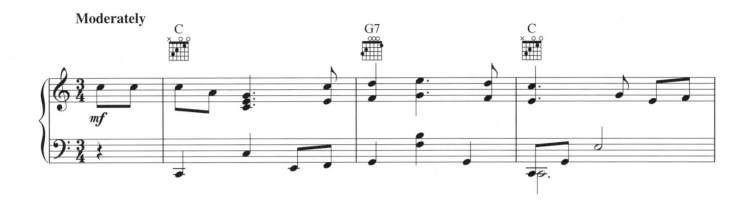

There's a line that's been drawn through the ag - es; _____
side march the forc - es of e - vil, _____
earth shakes with the force of the con - flict, _____

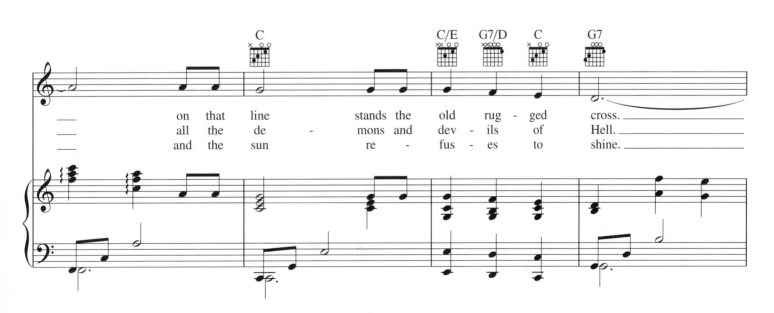

_____ on that line stands the old rug - ged cross. _____
_____ all the de - mons and dev - ils of Hell. _____
_____ and the sun re - fus - es to shine. _____

IT'S BEGINNING TO RAIN

Words by GLORIA GAITHER and AARON WILBURN
Music by WILLIAM J. GAITHER and AARON WILBURN

JESUS IS LORD OF ALL

Words and Music by WILLIAM J. and GLORIA GAITHER
Music by WILLIAM J. GAITHER

64

65

THE KING IS COMING

Words by WILLIAM J. and GLORIA GAITHER
and CHARLES MILLHUFF
Music by WILLIAM J. GAITHER

LET'S JUST PRAISE THE LORD

Words by WILLIAM J. and GLORIA GAITHER
Music by WILLIAM J. GAITHER

NOT BY MIGHT, NOT BY POWER

Words by GLORIA GAITHER
Music by WILLIAM J. GAITHER and CHRIS CHRISTIAN

REDEEMING LOVE

Words by GLORIA GAITHER
Music by WILLIAM J. GAITHER

SOMETHING BEAUTIFUL

Words by GLORIA GAITHER
Music by WILLIAM J. GAITHER

To Coda

strife, but He made some-thing ___ beau-ti-ful ___ of my life. ___ If there ev-er were dreams that were loft-y and no-ble, they were my dreams at the start. ___ And the hopes for life's best were the hopes that I har-bored

THANK GOD FOR THE PROMISE OF SPRING

Words by WILLIAM J. and GLORIA GAITHER
Music by WILLIAM J. GAITHER

THERE'S SOMETHING ABOUT THAT NAME

Words by WILLIAM J. and GLORIA GAITHER
Music by WILLIAM J. GAITHER

RECITATION

1. Jesus, the mere mention of His Name can calm the storm, heal the broken, raise the dead. At the Name of Jesus, I've seen sin-hardened men melted, derelicts transformed, the lights of hope put back into the eyes of a hopeless child...

At the Name of Jesus, hatred and bitterness turned to love and forgiveness, arguments cease.

I've heard a mother softly breathe His Name at the bedside of a child delirious from fever, and I've watched that little body grow quiet and the fevered brow cool.

I've sat beside a dying saint, her body racked with pain, who in those final fleeting seconds summoned her last ounce of ebbing strength to whisper earth's sweetest Name - Jesus, Jesus...

2. Emperors have tried to destroy it; philosophies have tried to stamp it out. Tyrants have tried to wash it from the face of the earth with the very blood of those who claimed it. Yet still it stands.

And there shall be that final day when every voice that has ever uttered a sound - every voice of Adam's race shall raise in one great mighty chorus to proclaim the Name of Jesus - for in that day "Every knee shall bow and every tongue shall confess that Jesus Chirst is Lord!!!"

Ah - so you see - it was not mere chance that caused the angel one night long ago to say to a virgin maiden, "His Name shall be called Jesus." Jesus - Jesus - Jesus. You know, there is something about that Name...

THIS IS THE TIME I MUST SING

Words by GLORIA GAITHER
Music by WILLIAM J. GAITHER

UPON THIS ROCK

Words by GLORIA GAITHER
Music by DONY McGUIRE

WE'LL BE THERE

Words by GLORIA GAITHER
Music by WILLIAM J. GAITHER

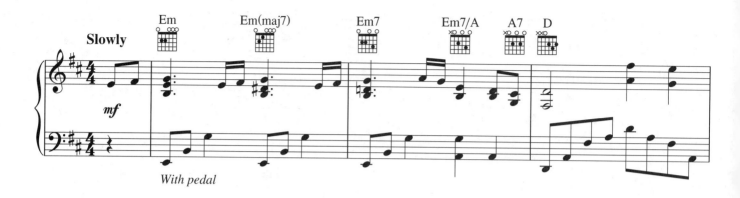

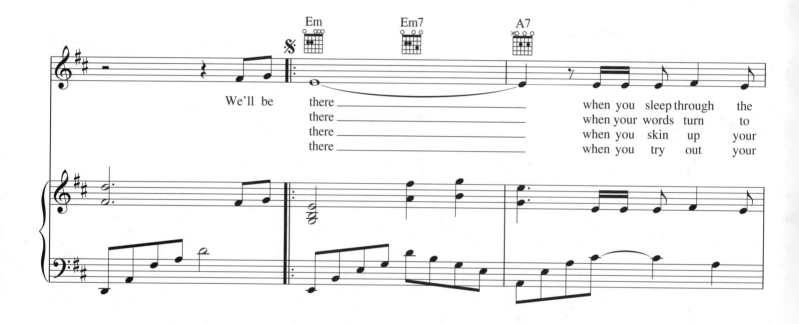

We'll be there ____ when you sleep through the
there ____ when your words turn to
there ____ when you skin up your
there ____ when you try out your

night. ____ We'll be there when you need us to
rhyme. ____ We'll be there, read you sto - ries at
knees. ____ We'll be there when you climb to the
wings. ____ We'll be there when you're ques - tion - ing

D.S. al Coda
(with repeat)

WORTHY THE LAMB

Words by WILLIAM J. and GLORIA GAITHER
Music by WILLIAM J. GAITHER

With a Worshipful Spirit

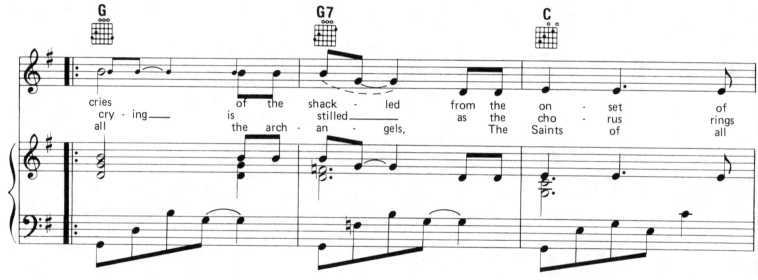

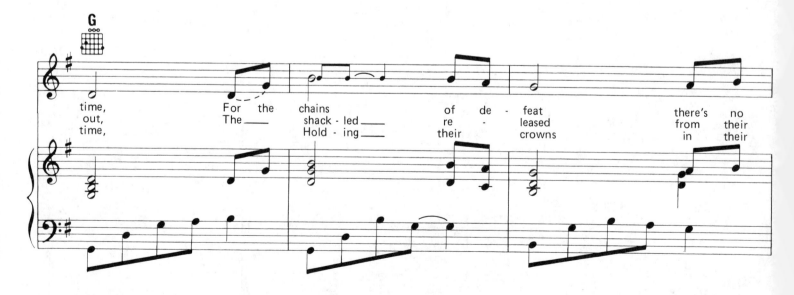